Lila and Andy learn about

Buildings

Revised & Updated Second Edition

Kenneth Adams

Book Cover by Kenneth Adams
Illustrations and Images by Kenneth Adams
Illustrations and Images created with AI Assistance
Second Edition 2025

ISBN: 978-1-998552-28-3

To my wife, your endless love and grace inspire me to be better.

To our kids, our greatest adventure, our forever motivation.

This book belongs to:

_____

Hi, my name is Lila. I'm twelve years old, and curls are kind of my thing. My hair might be wild, but I wouldn't have it any other way.

Sitting still? No thanks! I'm too busy creating my own world, one where anything is possible. I dream big and love telling stories that make people laugh, cry, or maybe even see the world in a whole new way.

My life is full of color, half-written stories, and creatures made out of anything you can imagine.

Hey there! I'm Andy, Lila's younger brother. I'm nine years old and consider myself practically an expert on all things awesome. Well, maybe not everything. But video games and computers? Those are my jam.

And the absolute coolest thing ever? Adventures! I'm always up for an adventure, especially the kind where we explore and discover new places or things!

So, are you ready? We're about to embark on an epic quest that will blow your mind. Let's do this!

Andy and I are a pretty awesome team, especially when it comes to exploring together! Today, we're going to share some awesome building knowledge we learned from our dad.

See, Dad's a structural engineer, which basically means he's the guy who figures out how to make buildings strong and safe, even when there's a blizzard or a hurricane!

Our Dad, "engineering".

Have you ever thought about why buildings stay strong even during a big storm? It's all thanks to engineers!

Engineers are kind of like problem-solvers who use science and math to create things that make our lives easier.

Structural engineers, like our dad, decide how many walls, columns, beams and floors a building needs to be safe and sturdy. That way, no matter how much it snows or how hard the wind blows, your house will stay standing tall!

Pretty cool, right?

Whether you live in a big city, a small town, or even on a farm in the countryside, you are surrounded by buildings, making the world a fun and interesting place.

Like silent guardians, buildings keep us safe and warm, a comforting hug from the world outside. From giant skyscrapers to cozy cabins, each structure has its own story to tell.

Buildings come in all shapes and sizes, each with a special job to do.

Houses shelter families, malls bustle with shops and restaurants, and schools, hospitals, and police stations serve and protect our communities.

Next time you see a building, imagine the stories unfolding within. Buildings are full of surprises just waiting to be discovered!

Ever wonder what goes into making those amazing buildings around us?

They're all built using special building blocks called building materials!

Let's explore some of the most common ones used to create these magnificent structures.

Concrete

Steel

Wood

Bricks

<u>Concrete</u> is a versatile building material that is used in many different parts of a building.

Concrete is made by mixing cement, sand, gravel, and water together. Once the ingredients are mixed, the concrete is poured into molds and left to dry and harden. When it's dry, concrete becomes as hard as a rock and very strong!

Engineers can make it even stronger by adding steel bars, called reinforcement, during the pouring process.

Another popular building material used in the construction of buildings is <u>steel</u>.

Steel is incredibly strong and can be made into many different shapes. This versatility allows engineers to design buildings in all sorts of creative ways.

Just like your bones hold up and give shape to your body, steel acts like the building's super-strong skeleton, providing both structure and form while holding everything together!

In regions rich with forests, where <u>wood</u> is plentiful, wood lumber becomes a natural building material.

Towering trees are carefully chopped from the forest and cut into long, flat planks at the sawmill. Once the planks are dry, they are cut into smaller sections, ready for use in construction.

Wood lumber is most commonly used for building homes and other residential structures, creating warm and inviting living spaces.

People have been using <u>bricks</u> to build structures for thousands of years, making them one of the oldest building materials in the world.

Made from concrete or clay, bricks are molded into various shapes and then dried or baked in an oven to become hard and strong.

During construction, bricks are stacked on top of each other and bonded together with a special glue called mortar.

Fire-resistant and durable, bricks can be used to build all sorts of structures, from houses and schools to churches, creating buildings that can last for many years.

Buildings are like giant puzzles, made up of many different parts.

The part of a building hidden below ground and impossible to see is called the substructure.

The part of the building you can see above ground is called the superstructure.

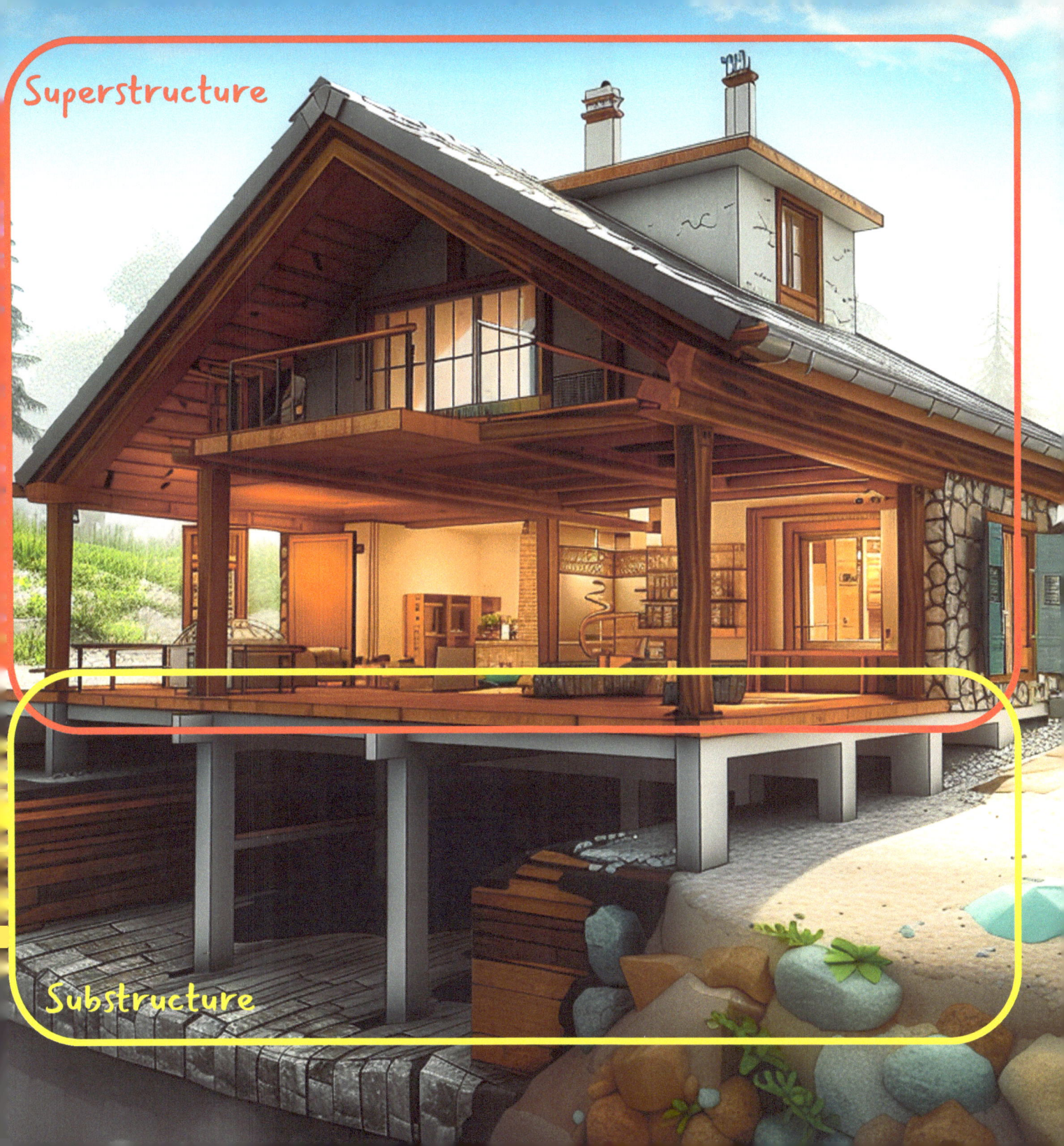

Superstructure

Substructure

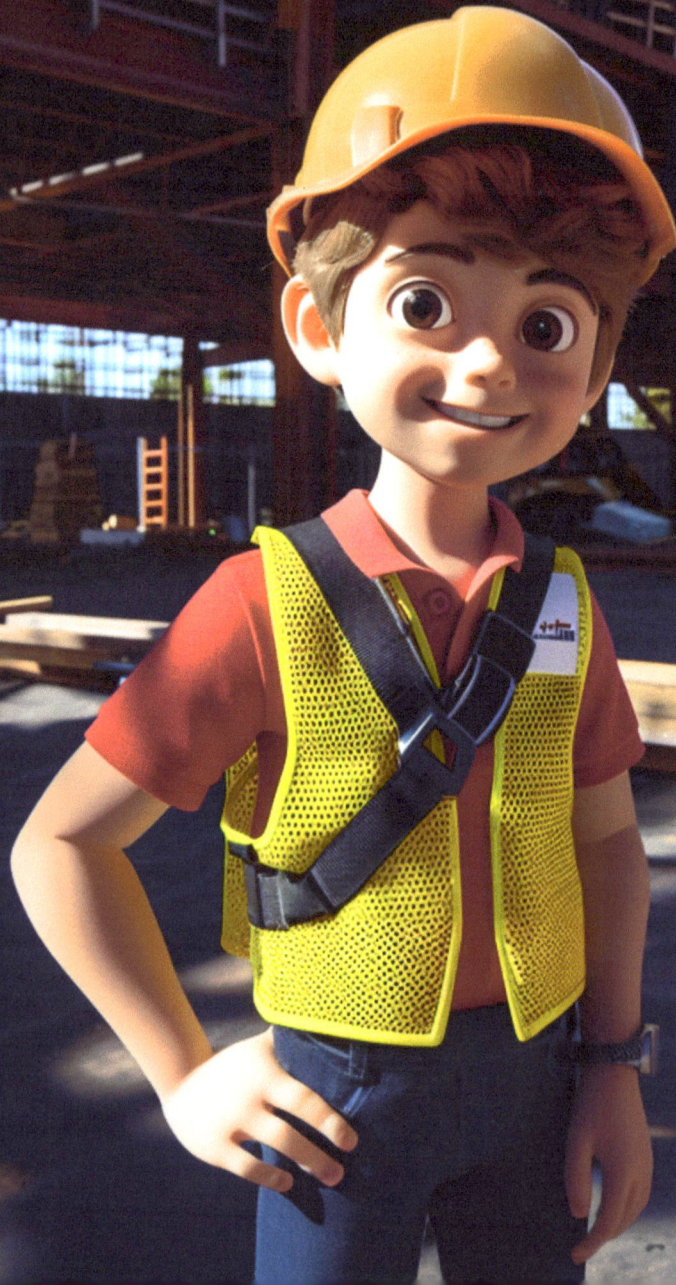

Part of the hidden underground substructure is called the <u>foundation</u>.

The foundation supports the building by spreading the weight of the building evenly, preventing it from sinking into the ground.

Foundations are made from concrete, steel, or even wood.

A concrete foundation under construction.

Buildings might look simple from the outside, but inside they're full of special parts that work together to form the frame of the building.

The frame gives the building its shape and strength.

Elements forming the frame, or superstructure, are typically made from steel, concrete, or wood.

<u>Walls</u> are the vertical parts of a building. These workhorses, made from concrete, brick, or steel, support the beams, floors, and roof, essentially holding everything up and forming the building's shell, keeping everybody inside safe and secure.

When buildings become really big and tall, they sometimes need help to carry the load. That's where <u>columns</u> come in! Like giant pillars standing tall inside the building, they act like super-strong legs, helping the walls hold up the structure above.

This wall forms the side of a house

A column supports the roof of this verandah

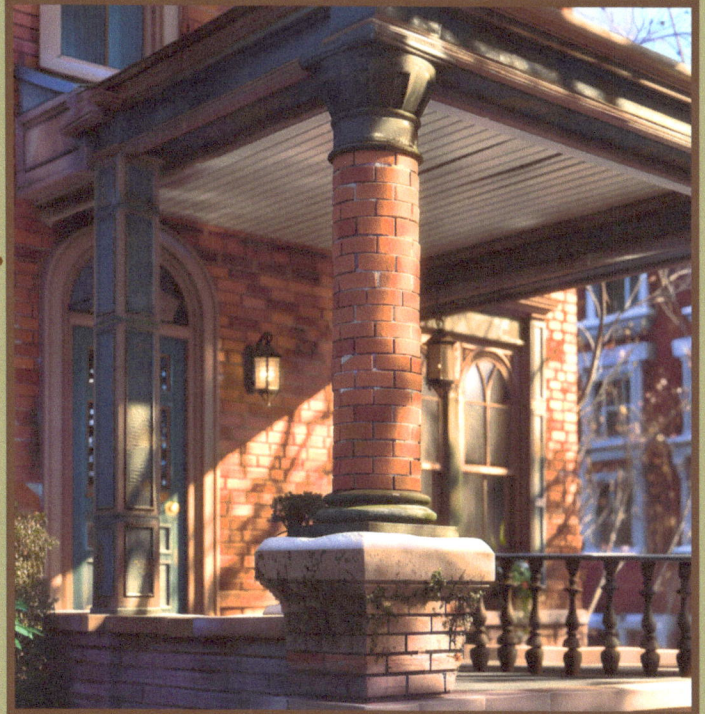

<u>Floors</u> are the flat surfaces inside buildings where we walk, jump, and play! They support and distribute the weight of people and furniture throughout the building.

Floors sometimes need help from special elements called beams! <u>Beams</u> are long, thin pieces that stretch across the walls and columns like bridges.

Floors and beams are the horizontal members of a building, and they work together to separate different levels within a building.

Both floors and beams can be made from concrete, wood, or steel.

The floor is the part on which we jump and play

Beams can help support the floor above, like a bridge

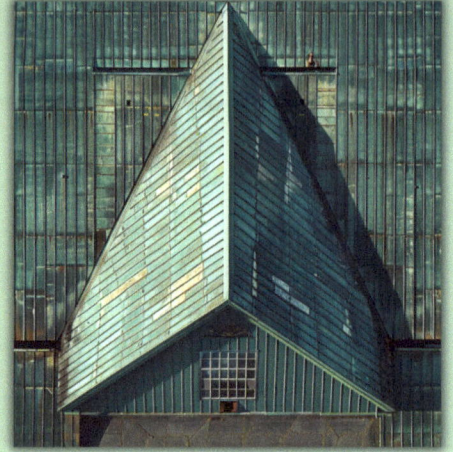

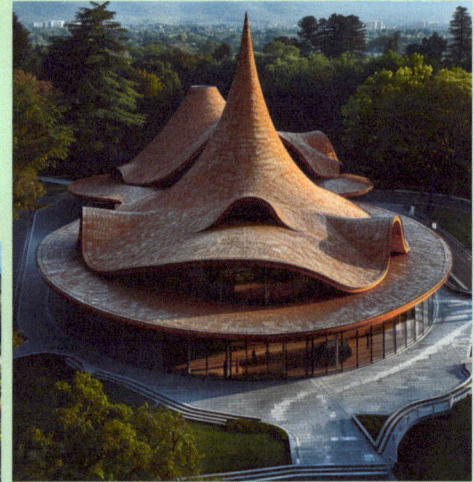

Every building needs a <u>roof</u>! This important part, like the building's hat, protects it from the elements, like rain, snow, and the sun.

Roofs come in all shapes and sizes, flat, slanted, or even curved, depending on the design and style of the building. They're the final piece of the puzzle, ensuring the building stays warm, comfortable, and dry.

A roof can be made from wood, metal, or concrete, and is usually covered with tiles or shingles.

Engineers design buildings to resist invisible forces called _loads_, which come in different forms.

Dead loads are the weight of everything that's always there, like the walls and floors.

Live loads are the weights of things that come and go, like people walking around or furniture being moved.

Environmental loads are the forces buildings face from Mother Nature, like strong winds trying to push them over, or the weight of heavy snow. Even earthquakes can be a load that engineers have to consider!

The next time you see a building, imagine all the different forces it silently battles!

Now that we know all the different parts of a building, and how engineers design them, let's see how they all come together to create amazing structures!

Building construction is like following a giant recipe, with each step happening in a specific order. Construction workers form a team, working together to bring buildings to life!

First, before they start building, construction workers prepare the ground using big machines like bulldozers and excavators. Then they pour the concrete foundation, creating a super-strong platform for everything else to sit on.

Next comes the frame! Workers use cranes and other big machines to put up the building's skeleton, which can be made from steel, concrete, or wood, depending on what type of building they're constructing. This is probably my favorite part because those cranes are massive and can lift almost anything!

Once the frame is ready, workers add the floors, walls, and roof, turning the skeleton into a real building that can keep the weather out. Finally, they add windows, doors, and all the details that make the building ready for people to use.

Everyone on a construction site wears hard hats and safety gear to stay safe. Safety first, adventure second! Watching a building come together piece by piece is pretty amazing.

Wow! We learned so much about buildings, from skyscrapers reaching for the clouds to cozy homes on quiet streets. There are so many amazing buildings in the world, each one unique!

Next time you see a construction site, imagine all the hard work that goes into making that building come to life, brick by brick, wall by wall, floor by floor. And who knows, maybe one day you'll become an engineer and get to design your very own Super Structure!

Buildings
Careers

If you care about creating amazing structures and are curious about solving the challenges of building safe, strong, and beautiful places where people live, work, and play, then careers dedicated to Buildings might be perfect for you! There are many exciting jobs for people who want to help create the structures that shape our world. Here are examples of careers that work together to make buildings come to life.

<u>Architects</u> create the overall design and look of buildings. Architects draw detailed plans and make sure buildings are both beautiful and functional.

<u>Structural Engineers</u> use science and math to make sure buildings are strong and safe, even during storms and earthquakes.

<u>Civil Engineers</u> plan and design the infrastructure around buildings, like roads, bridges, and water systems.

<u>Project Managers</u> coordinate all the different aspects of construction projects, making sure everything happens on time and within budget.

<u>Interior Designers</u> design the inside spaces of buildings to make them beautiful, comfortable, and functional. They choose colors, furniture, lighting, and layouts that make people feel good in the space.

<u>Surveyors</u> measure and map the land before construction begins. Surveyors use special instruments to determine property boundaries and make sure buildings are built in exactly the right spot.

Construction Managers and General Contractors oversee the entire building project. They coordinate all the different workers, make sure materials arrive on time, and ensure the building gets completed safely and on schedule.

Carpenters or Framers build the wooden parts of structures, including frames, floors, and roofs. Carpenters are skilled at measuring, cutting, and joining wood pieces together to create strong building components.

Electricians install all the electrical systems that bring power and lighting to buildings. They wire buildings so you can flip a switch and turn on lights or plug in your devices.

Plumbers install the water and sewer systems that bring clean water in and take waste water out. Without plumbers, buildings wouldn't have working bathrooms, kitchens, or drinking fountains.

HVAC Technicians install and maintain heating, ventilation, and air conditioning systems that keep buildings comfortable year-round. They make sure buildings stay warm in winter and cool in summer.

Masons or Bricklayers specialize in building with bricks, stones, and concrete blocks. These skilled workers create beautiful and durable walls that can last for hundreds of years.

Heavy Equipment Operators drive and operate big machines like bulldozers, excavators, and dump trucks. These operators prepare construction sites and move materials around the job site.

Crane Operators operate those massive cranes that can lift heavy materials high into the air. Crane operators need excellent coordination and focus to move materials around construction sites safely.

Building Inspectors check buildings during and after construction to make sure they meet safety codes and are built correctly. Inspectors help keep everyone safe by ensuring buildings are constructed properly.

Construction Safety Managers make sure everyone on construction sites follows safety rules and wears proper protective equipment. They train workers and investigate any accidents to prevent future injuries.

Construction Estimators calculate how much materials and labor will cost for building projects. They help determine budgets and make sure construction projects stay affordable.

Facility Managers oversee the day-to-day operations of large buildings like schools, hospitals, or office buildings. They coordinate maintenance, security, and services to keep buildings functioning properly.

Buildings Glossary

A <u>glossary</u> is like a mini-dictionary of terms with definitions.

Here's a glossary of terms associated with <u>Buildings</u>.

<u>Architect</u> - A person who designs buildings and creates the plans that show what the building will look like. Architects work with engineers to make sure their designs are both beautiful and safe!

<u>Beam</u> - A long, strong piece that stretches across walls and columns like a bridge. Beams help support floors and roofs, and can be made from wood, steel, or concrete.

<u>Blueprint</u> - Detailed drawings that show exactly how to build a structure. Think of blueprints as the instruction manual for construction workers!

<u>Brick</u> - Small blocks made from clay or concrete that are baked until hard. Bricks have been used to build structures for thousands of years and are stacked together with mortar to create walls.

<u>Building Code</u> - Rules that tell builders how to construct safe buildings. These rules make sure all buildings can protect people during storms, earthquakes, and fires.

<u>Building Materials</u> - The special building blocks used to create structures, like concrete, steel, wood, and bricks.

<u>Column</u> - A tall, strong pillar that stands inside buildings to help support heavy loads. Columns act like super-strong legs, helping walls hold up everything above them.

<u>Concrete</u> - A building material made by mixing cement, sand, gravel, and water. When it dries, concrete becomes as hard as rock and incredibly strong!

<u>Construction Site</u> - The place where a building is being built. Construction sites are busy places filled with workers, machines, and building materials.

<u>Contractor</u> - The person who manages the construction project and makes sure everything gets built correctly and safely.

<u>Crane</u> - A massive machine that can lift and move heavy building materials like steel beams. Some cranes are so tall they can reach the clouds!

<u>Dead Load</u> - The weight of everything in a building that stays in the same place, like walls, floors, and the roof.

<u>Demolition</u> - The process of carefully tearing down old buildings to make room for new ones.

<u>Environmental Load</u> - Forces that buildings face from Mother Nature, like strong winds, heavy snow, or earthquakes.

<u>Excavator</u> - A big machine with a giant arm and bucket that digs holes and moves dirt around construction sites.

<u>Floor</u> - The flat surface inside buildings where people walk, run, and play. Floors support the weight of people and furniture.

<u>Foundation</u> - The hidden part of a building that goes underground. The foundation spreads the weight of the building evenly so it won't sink into the ground.

<u>Frame</u> - The skeleton of a building that gives it shape and strength. Frames can be made from steel, concrete, or wood.

<u>Hard Hat</u> - A special helmet that construction workers wear to protect their heads from falling objects.

<u>Insulation</u> - Special material placed inside walls and roofs to keep buildings warm in winter and cool in summer.

<u>Live Load</u> - The weight of things that come and go in a building, like people walking around or furniture being moved.

<u>Load</u> - The weight or force that pushes on a building. Engineers design buildings to handle many different types of loads.

Mortar - A special glue that holds bricks together when building walls.

Reinforcement - Steel bars that are added to concrete to make it even stronger. The steel and concrete work together like a super team!

Renovation - Fixing up or improving an old building to make it better or more modern.

Roof - The top part of a building that protects everything inside from rain, snow, and sun. Roofs are like the building's hat!

Safety Gear - Special clothing and equipment that construction workers wear to stay safe, including hard hats, safety goggles, and bright vests.

Scaffolding - Temporary metal structures that workers climb on to reach high places when building or fixing structures.

Skyscraper - A very tall building that seems to touch the sky. Skyscrapers are engineering marvels that can have hundreds of floors!

Steel - An incredibly strong metal that can be shaped in many different ways. Steel acts like a building's super-strong skeleton.

Structural Engineer - A person who uses science and math to figure out how to make buildings strong and safe, even during storms and earthquakes.

Substructure - The part of a building that's hidden underground, including the foundation.

Superstructure - The part of a building that you can see above ground, including walls, floors, and the roof.

Wall - The vertical parts of a building that form the building's shell and help support floors and roofs. Walls keep everyone inside safe and secure.

Wood Lumber - Building material made from trees that are cut into flat planks. Wood is often used to build homes and create warm, inviting spaces.

Buildings Quiz

Multiple Choice (Choose the best answer)

1. What is Lila and Andy's dad's job?
   a) Architect
   b) Construction worker
   c) Structural engineer
   d) Building inspector

2. Which building material is made by mixing cement, sand, gravel, and water?
   a) Steel
   b) Concrete
   c) Wood lumber
   d) Brick

3. What do engineers add to concrete to make it even stronger?
   a) More water
   b) Steel bars called reinforcement
   c) Extra cement
   d) Sand

4. Steel acts like a building's:
   a) Hat
   b) Shoes
   c) Super-strong skeleton
   d) Coat

5. Where does wood lumber come from?
   a) Factories
   b) Mines
   c) Towering trees from forests
   d) Steel mills

6. How long have people been using bricks to build structures?
    a) Hundreds of years
    b) Thousands of years
    c) Decades
    d) Since yesterday

7. What holds bricks together during construction?
    a) Glue
    b) Tape
    c) Mortar
    d) Water

8. The part of a building hidden below ground is called the:
    a) Superstructure
    b) Substructure
    c) Frame
    d) Foundation

9. What does the foundation do?
    a) Keeps rain out
    b) Provides electricity
    c) Spreads the building's weight evenly
    d) Decorates the building

10. The frame of a building gives it:
    a) Color and style
    b) Windows and doors
    c) Shape and strength
    d) Heat and air conditioning

11. Walls are the _____ parts of a building.
    a) Horizontal
    b) Vertical
    c) Curved
    d) Triangular

12. When buildings become really big and tall. what helps carry the load?
    a) Beams
    b) Columns
    c) Roofs
    d) Windows

13. What are floors and beams called in building terms?
    a) Vertical members
    b) Horizontal members
    c) Diagonal members
    d) Circular members

14. The roof protects buildings from:
    a) People
    b) Cars
    c) Rain. snow. and sun
    d) Other buildings

15. What is the first step in building construction?
    a) Adding the roof
    b) Installing windows
    c) Preparing the ground
    d) Painting the walls

16. What machines help prepare the ground for construction?
    a) Cranes and forklifts
    b) Bulldozers and excavators
    c) Trucks and cars
    d) Helicopters and planes

17. Dead loads are the weight of things that:
    a) Are always there
    b) Come and go
    c) Fall from the sky
    d) Move around constantly

18. Live loads include the weight of:
    a) Walls and floors
    b) The roof and foundation
    c) People and furniture
    d) Rain and snow

19. Environmental loads come from:
    a) People inside the building
    b) Mother Nature
    c) Construction workers
    d) Building materials

20. What safety equipment do construction workers wear?
    a) Regular clothes
    b) Swimming gear
    c) Hard hats and safety gear
    d) Party costumes

21. Which machine can lift things that weigh as much as elephants?
   a) Bulldozer
   b) Excavator
   c) Truck
   d) Crane

22. Buildings act like _____ that keep us safe and warm.
   a) Silent guardians
   b) Loud machines
   c) Moving vehicles
   d) Flying objects

23. What covers roofs to protect them?
   a) Paint
   b) Tiles or shingles
   c) Plastic wrap
   d) Paper

24. The part of the building you can see above ground is called the:
   a) Substructure
   b) Foundation
   c) Superstructure
   d) Basement

25. Houses, schools, and hospitals are examples of:
   a) Transportation
   b) Buildings with special jobs
   c) Natural formations
   d) Weather patterns

Fill-in-the-Blank

26. Lila is _____ years old and curls are kind of her thing.

27. Andy is _____ years old and considers himself an expert on video games and computers.

28. A structural engineer uses _____ and _____ to create things that make our lives easier.

29. Buildings keep us safe and warm like a comforting _____ from the world outside.

30. Concrete becomes as hard as a _____ when it dries.

31. _____ lumber is most commonly used for building homes and other residential structures.

32. Bricks are bonded together with a special glue called _____.

33. The foundation prevents buildings from _____ into the ground.

34. Columns act like super-strong _____, helping walls hold up the structure above.

35. Beams stretch across walls and columns like _____.

36. The roof is like the building's _____ that protects it from the elements.

37. Engineers design buildings to resist invisible forces called _____.

38. _____ loads are the weights of things that come and go.

39. Strong winds and heavy snow are examples of _____ loads.

40. Construction workers prepare the ground using big machines like _____ and _____.

41. The building's _____ holds everything together and gives the building its shape.

42. Workers add _____, _____, and _____ to turn the skeleton into a real building.

43. Everyone on a construction site wears _____ _____ to stay safe.

44. Buildings are like giant _____, made up of many different parts.

45. The _____ supports the building by spreading its weight evenly.

46. Elements forming the frame are typically made from _____, _____, or _____.

47. Roofs can be _____, _____, or even _____ depending on the building's design.

48. Trees are cut into long, flat _____ at the sawmill.

49. Bricks are made from _____ or _____.

50. The frame gives the building its _____ and _____.

<u>True/False (Write T for True or F for False)</u>

51. Lila is older than Andy.

52. Andy loves adventures and exploring new places.

53. Structural engineers only work on small buildings.

54. Steel can be made into many different shapes.

55. Concrete is made by mixing only cement and water.

56. Wood lumber creates warm and inviting living spaces.

57. Bricks are fire-resistant and durable.

58. The substructure is the part of the building you can see above ground.

59. Foundations can be made from concrete, steel, or wood.

60. Walls are horizontal parts of a building.

61. All buildings need columns to carry the load.

62. Floors and beams work together to separate different levels in a building.

63. Every building needs a roof.

64. Dead loads include people walking around.

65. Environmental loads can include earthquakes.

66. Construction follows a specific order of steps.

67. Bulldozers are used to lift heavy steel beams.

68. Safety gear is optional on construction sites.

69. Cranes can lift things that weigh as much as elephants.

70. Buildings come in only one shape and size.

Quiz Answer Key

Multiple Choice	Fill-in-the-Blank	True/False
1. c	26. twelve	51. True
2. b	27. nine	52. True
3. b	28. science, math	53. False
4. c	29. hug	54. True
5. c	30. rock	55. False
6. b	31. Wood	56. True
7. c	32. mortar	57. True
8. b	33. sinking	58. False
9. c	34. legs	59. True
10. c	35. bridges	60. False
11. b	36. hat	61. False
12. b	37. loads	62. True
13. b	38. Live	63. True
14. c	39. environmental	64. False
15. c	40. bulldozers, excavators	65. True
16. b	41. frame (or skeleton)	66. True
17. a	42. floors, walls, roof	67. False
18. c	43. hard hats (or safety gear)	68. False
19. b	44. puzzles	69. True
20. c	45. foundation	70. False
21. d	46. steel, concrete, wood	
22. a	47. flat, slanted, curved	
23. b	48. planks	
24. c	49. concrete, clay	
25. b	50. shape, strength	

Take a look at other subjects Lila and Andy are learning about...

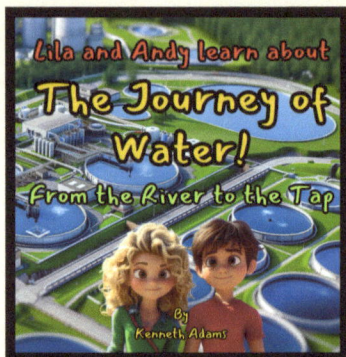

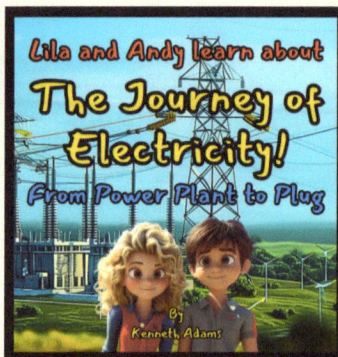

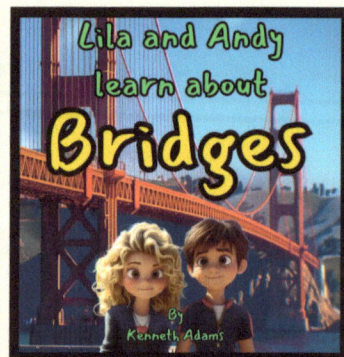

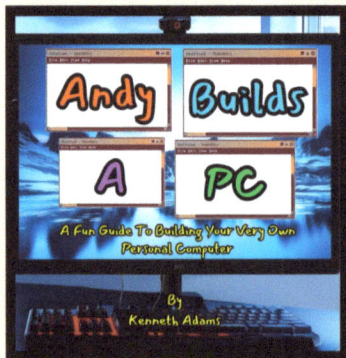

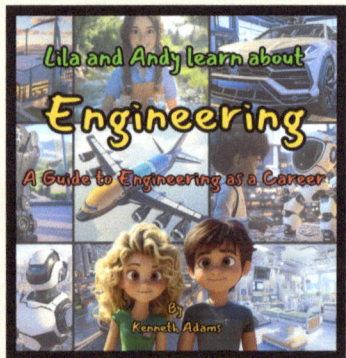

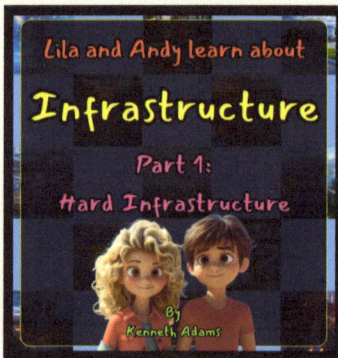

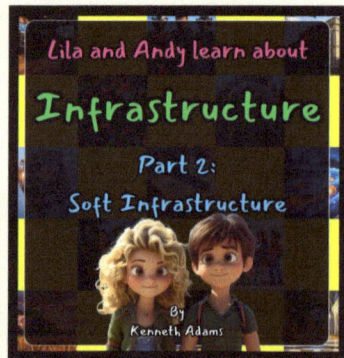

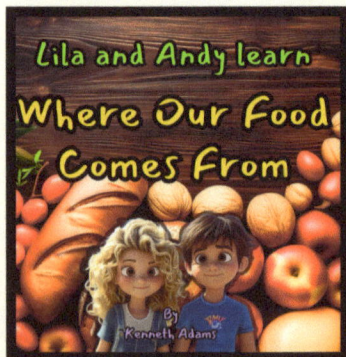

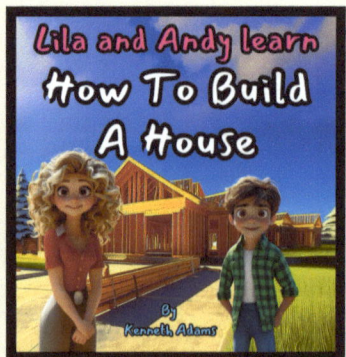

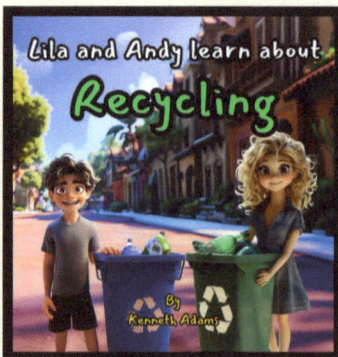

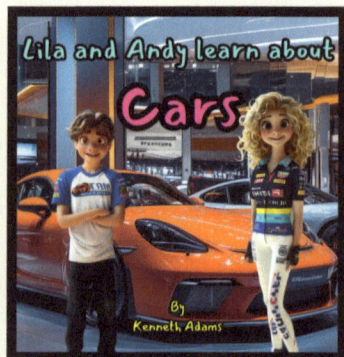

Lila and Andy learn about **The Journey of Water!** From the River to the Tap
By Kenneth Adams

Lila and Andy learn **What happens when you Flush!** How Wastewater gets clean again
By Kenneth Adams

Lila and Andy learn about **The Journey of Electricity!** From Power Plant to Plug
By Kenneth Adams

Lila and Andy learn about **Bridges**
By Kenneth Adams

Andy Builds A PC A Fun Guide To Building Your Very Own Personal Computer
By Kenneth Adams

Lila and Andy learn about **Engineering** A Guide to Engineering as a Career
By Kenneth Adams

Lila and Andy learn about **Infrastructure** Part 1: Hard Infrastructure
By Kenneth Adams

Lila and Andy learn about **Infrastructure** Part 2: Soft Infrastructure
By Kenneth Adams

Lila and Andy learn **Where Our Food Comes From**
By Kenneth Adams

Lila and Andy learn **How To Build A House**
By Kenneth Adams

Lila and Andy learn about **Recycling**
By Kenneth Adams

Lila and Andy learn about **Cars**
By Kenneth Adams

Lila and Andy learn about Safety on Ice
By Kenneth Adams

Lila and Andy learn about Winter Roads
By Kenneth Adams

Lila and Andy learn about Smart Cities
By Kenneth Adams

Lila and Andy learn about Digital Networks
How the Internet Connects Us
By Kenneth Adams

Lila and Andy learn about Biomimicry
Kenneth Adams

Lila and Andy learn about Artificial Intelligence
Discover Large Language Models and Prompt Engineering
by Kenneth Adams

Lila and Andy learn about Climate Change
Understand Our Changing Planet
Kenneth Adams

Lila and Andy learn about Environmental Science
Protecting Earth Through Science
Kenneth Adams

Lila and Andy learn about The Carbon Cycle
Kenneth Adams

Lila and Andy learn about Data Science & Cryptography
Kenneth Adams

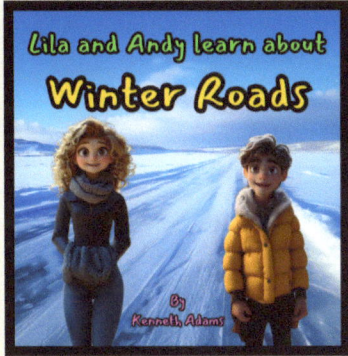

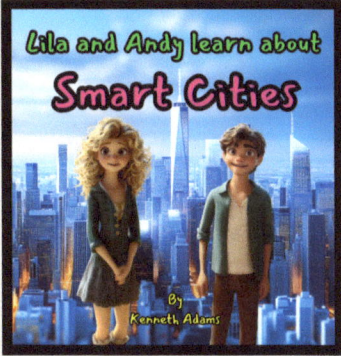

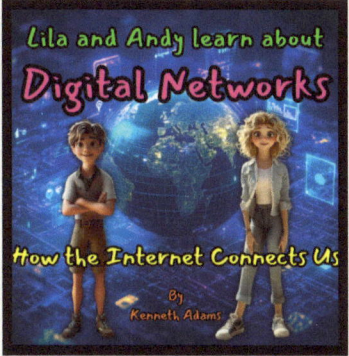

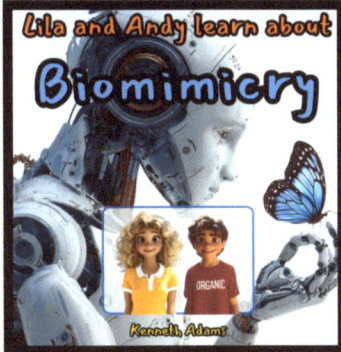

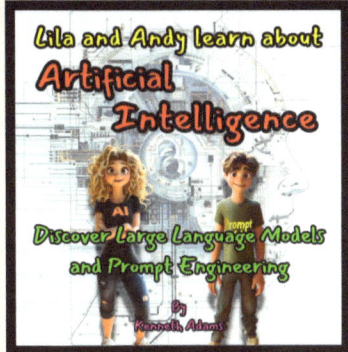

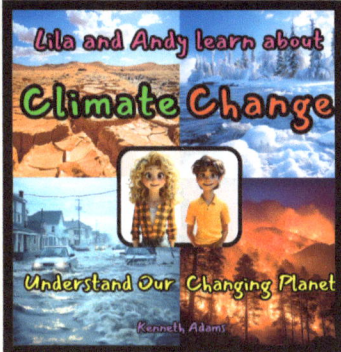

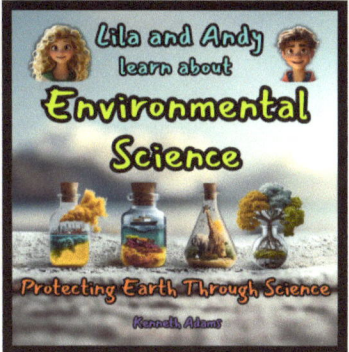

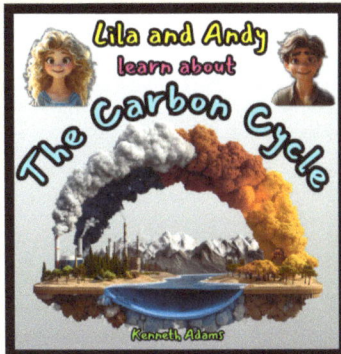

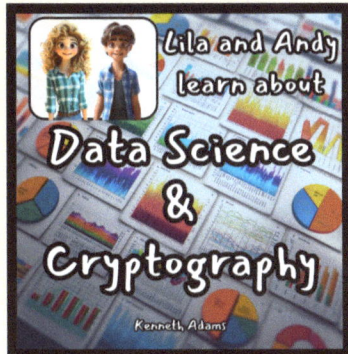

Available on Amazon.

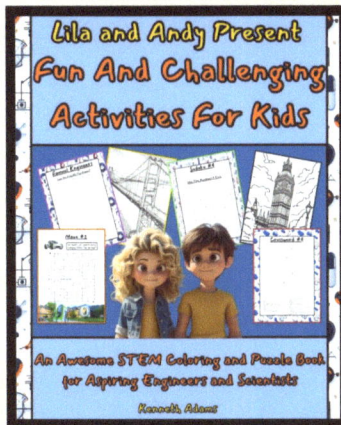

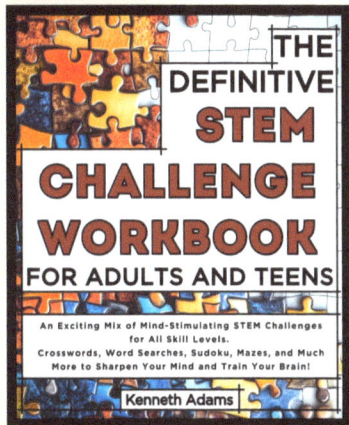

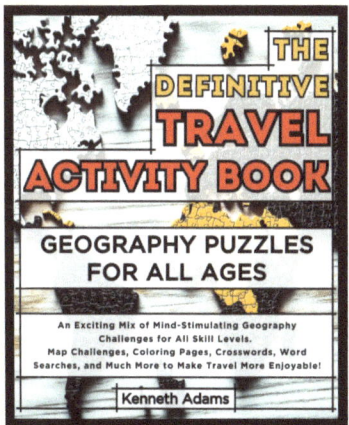

Lila and Andy Present Fun And Challenging Activities For Kids
An Awesome STEM Coloring and Puzzle Book for Aspiring Engineers and Scientists
Kenneth Adams

THE DEFINITIVE STEM CHALLENGE WORKBOOK FOR ADULTS AND TEENS
An Exciting Mix of Mind-Stimulating STEM Challenges for All Skill Levels.
Crosswords, Word Searches, Sudoku, Mazes, and Much More to Sharpen Your Mind and Train Your Brain!
Kenneth Adams

THE DEFINITIVE TRAVEL ACTIVITY BOOK
GEOGRAPHY PUZZLES FOR ALL AGES
An Exciting Mix of Mind-Stimulating Geography Challenges for All Skill Levels.
Map Challenges, Coloring Pages, Crosswords, Word Searches, and Much More to Make Travel More Enjoyable!
Kenneth Adams

www.ingramcontent.com/pod-product-compliance
Lightning Source LLC
Chambersburg PA
CBHW040032110426
42737CB00053B/91